THE WAR OF THE POOR

And the twenty-four gentlemen present at the palace of the President of the Reichstag that February 20 are none other than their proxies, the clergy of major industry; they are the high priests of Ptah. And there they stand, affectless, like twenty-four calculating machines at the gates of Hell.

ÉRIC VUILLARD is an award-winning author and filmmaker who has written ten books, including *Conquistadors* (winner of the 2010 Prix Ignatius J. Reilly), and *La bataille d'Occident* and *Congo* (both of which received the 2012 Prix Franz-Hessel and the 2013 Prix Valery-Larbaud). He won the 2017 Prix Goncourt, France's most prestigious literary prize, for *The Order of the Day* (Other Press, 2018). Born in Lyon in 1968, he now lives in Rennes, France.

MARK POLIZZOTTI has translated more than fifty books from the French, including works by Gustave Flaubert, Patrick Modiano, Marguerite Duras, André Breton, and Raymond Roussel. A Chevalier of the Ordre des Arts et des Lettres and the recipient of a 2016 American Academy of Arts & Letters Award for Literature, he is the author of eleven books. He directs the publications program at the Metropolitan Museum of Art in New York.

OTHER PRESS
New York

THE
WAR
OF THE
POOR

ÉRIC VUILLARD

Translated from the French by Mark Polizzotti

Copyright © Actes Sud, 2019
Originally published in French as *La guerre des pauvres*
in 2019 by Actes Sud, Arles, France
Translation copyright © Mark Polizzotti, 2020
Published by arrangement with Actes Sud and 2 Seas Literary Agency

The translator gratefully acknowledges previously published English versions of
Thomas Müntzer's writings, in *Thomas Müntzer – Writings and Letters*, trans. Andy
Drummond; Thomas Müntzer, *Sermon to the Princes*, trans. Michael G. Baylor; and
Friedrich Engels, *The Peasant War in Germany*, trans. Moissaye J. Olgin et al.

Production editor: Yvonne E. Cárdenas
Text designer: Jennifer Daddio / Bookmark Design & Media Inc.
This book was set in Adobe Garamond Pro and Trajan
by Alpha Design & Composition of Pittsfield, NH

1 3 5 7 9 10 8 6 4 2

Library of Congress Cataloging-in-Publication Data
Names: Vuillard, Éric, author. | Polizzotti, Mark, translator.
Title: The War of the Poor / Éric Vuillard ; translated from the French
by Mark Polizzotti.
Other titles: Guerre des pauvres. English
Description: New York : Other Press, [2020]
Identifiers: LCCN 2020029868 (print) | LCCN 2020029869 (ebook) |
ISBN 9781635420081 (hardcover) | ISBN 9781635420098 (ebook)
Subjects: LCSH: Münzer, Thomas, approximately 1490-1525. | Peasants' War,
1524-1525. | Reformation—Germany—Biography.
Classification: LCC BX4946.M8 V8513 2020 (print) | LCC BX4946.M8 (ebook) |
DDC 843/.914—dc23
LC record available at https://lccn.loc.gov/2020029868
LC ebook record available at https://lccn.loc.gov/2020029869

CONTENTS

THE WAR OF THE POOR

THE STORY OF
THOMAS MÜNTZER

His father had been hanged. Dropped into the void like a sack of feed. They'd had to carry him on their shoulders at night; then he made not a sound, his mouth full of earth. After that, everything had caught fire. The oaks, the fields, the rivers, the white bedstraw on the embankment, the barren soil, the church, everything. He was eleven years old.

At age fifteen, he had formed a secret league to oppose the Archbishop of Magdeburg and the Church of Rome. He read the *Epistles of Clement*, the *Martyrdom of Polycarp*, Papias's *Fragments*. With several comrades, he praised God's marvels, crossed the Jordan in a dressing gown; afterward he traced the cosmic wheel (a sign of assembly) on the ground in chalk and they each lay on it in turns, arms outstretched, so that Heaven might descend to Earth. And then he remembered the corpse of his father, the enormous tongue like a single, desiccated word. "I was filled with joy, but one unites with God only through terrible suffering and despair." That's what he believed.

They say that in Stolberg, there was a vintner by the name of Barthol Munzer. And they still talk about a Monczer Berld and a Monczers Merth, but nothing is known about them. There is also a Thomas Miinzer, killed in a bar brawl. We don't know if he got hit in the face with a fist or a log, nor do we know if he was related to Thomas Müntzer, the one whose father, around 1500, for reasons unknown, was executed on the orders of the count of Stolberg—some say hanged, others say burned.

Fifty years earlier, a molten substance had flowed, flowed from Mainz over the rest of Europe, flowed between the hills of every town, between the letters of every name, in the gutters, between every twist and turn of thought; and every letter, every fragment of an idea, every punctuation mark had found itself cast in a bit of metal. They had arranged them in wooden trays. Hands had plucked out one, then another, and composed words, lines, pages. They had moistened them with ink and a great force had slowly pressed the letters onto paper. They had repeated this procedure dozens and dozens of times, before folding the sheets into signatures of four, or eight, or sixteen pages. They had put them in sequence, glued them together, sewn them, bound them in leather. They had made a book. The Bible.

And so, in the space of three years, they had made one hundred eighty copies, where in that time a single monk could have made only one. And then the books had multiplied like maggots in a corpse.

Now, young Thomas Müntzer read the Bible, grew up with Ezekiel, Hosea, Daniel; but they were Gutenberg's Ezekiel, Gutenberg's Hosea, Gutenberg's Daniel. And after passing through the rotten, yawning gate that scraped the ground, he spent long hours downstairs in the old kitchen, rubbing his eyes. He didn't know what he was seeing or what he was supposed to see. He was solitary like a thief, and innocent.

Time passed. He lived with his mother, no doubt frugally. His heart hurt. Beneath the oaks, the pines, on the poor soil of the Harz Mountains, as he chased after pigs with the other children, he must have suddenly stopped short, alone, feeling foolish, and wept. Yes, I imagine him on the edge of a river of small black pebbles, the Wipper, perhaps, or the Krebsbach, no matter; or else on the flanks of sad little summits of chaotic rock, eroded

cliffs, shabby peat bogs, in the Bode or Oker val-
ley, suffocating in a mix of bitterness and love.

Finally, he enrolled as a student in Leipzig,
then became a priest in Halberstadt and Bruns-
wick, then a provost here and there, then, after
considerable tribulations among the Lutherite
plebeians, he emerged from his hole in 1520, when
he was named a preacher in Zwickau.

ZWICKAU

Outside the borders of Saxony, hardly anyone knows Zwickau. It's just another backwater. *Zwicker* means pince-nez; *Zwickel* means gusset; *Zwiebel*, onion; and *zwiebeln*, to harass or bully. But Zwickau means nothing, or else it means onionskin, poor slobs, good business, yes, that's what Zwickau means: poor slobs and good business. For in Zwickau they wove, they wove a lot, they wove for the whole world, for people in

Frankfurt and Dresden; back then, they say, even in Paris some people slept on Zwickau sheets. And on top of that, in Zwickau they dug the earth, exploited the mines. And so, right after the Welsers and the Fuggers come the burghers of Zwickau.

The burghers heard Müntzer preach at St. Mary's church, as a temporary replacement for Johann Sylvanus Egranus. When Egranus returned, they appointed Müntzer to St. Katharine's, a parish of weavers and miners. There, he mixed with the Zwickau reformists Nikolaus Storch, Mark Stübner, and Thomas Drechsel. That shadowy trio was raising holy hell, wallowing in ecstasy, visions, and dreams, waiting for those moments when the Good Lord would speak to them *directly*. The great squabble was over whether or not to advocate voluntary, conscious baptism. Oh, it might sound a bit old-fashioned, this notion of baptism, this rationalism of lunatics, this *Aufklärung* of cruets. But it was a reaction to corruption in the Church, the irrationality of the doctrine and the sacraments. For the lunatics of Zwickau were reading something other than Saint Augustine and Thomas Aquinas; they were reading Erasmus and Nicholas of Cusa, Raymond Lully and Jan Hus. They debated, argued, yearned to stand naked before the Truth.

And so the city was divided. On one side were the patricians of St. Mary's, on the other the plebeians of St. Katharine's. Reason and purity would be for the poor. It was before them that Müntzer began to agitate; it was there that his wound intensified. He spoke. They listened. He cited the Gospels: "You cannot serve both God and money." He believed he could read the scriptures simply, take them literally. He believed in a pure, authentic Christianity. He believed it was all set down in black and white in Saint Paul, that all the essentials could be found in the Gospels. That's what he believed.

And this is what he preached to the poor weavers and miners, to their wives, to the destitute of Zwickau. He quoted the Gospels and added exclamation points. And they listened to him. And passions began to stir, for those weavers knew full well that if you pulled at a thread the whole tapestry would unravel; the miners knew that if you dug deep enough, the whole tunnel would collapse. And so they began to realize they'd been lied to. They had long felt troubled and afflicted; there were many things they didn't understand. They had a hard time understanding why God, the God of beggars, crucified between two thieves, needed such pomp. Why his ministers needed luxury of such embarrassing proportions. Why the God of the poor was so strangely on the side of the rich, always with the rich. Why his words about giving up everything issued from the mouths of those who had taken everything.

GOD AND THE PEOPLE
SPEAK THE SAME
LANGUAGE

After less than a year, Müntzer was forced to leave Zwickau. He then went to Bohemia. The place was in ferment. They were still reeling from the Great Schism. Heresy was rampant. A yearning for purity swept over the land, galvanized the masses, cut short the tired old chatter. Suddenly, the Sprit entered people's homes. At night, frogs croaked an unnameable truth: They would name it. The vulture's beak gnawed on the flesh of corpses: They would make it speak. And so it followed that the Bible should be accessible to human reason. That great leap had first been made in England, two centuries earlier. It was John Wycliffe who had the idea—just a tiny idea, barely a notion, but one that would make a huge noise—that there exists a direct relationship between men and God. From that initial idea, it logically followed that anyone could guide themselves using the scriptures. And that second idea led to a third: The clergy is no longer necessary. Ergo: The Bible had to be translated into English. Wycliffe—who evidently was not short on ideas—had two or three more terrifying thoughts, such as proposing that popes be chosen by drawing lots. In his fervor, now a hairbreadth from madness, he declared that slavery was a sin. Then he averred that the clergy should take a vow of poverty. After that, to really piss people off, he repudiated transubstantiation as a mental aberration. And as the icing on the cake, his most terrifying idea of all, he preached the equality of all human beings.

There followed a rain of papal bulls. The pope got mad, and when a pope gets mad, it rains bulls. Translate the Vulgate into English? How awful! Today, the lowliest user's guide is in English; they speak English everywhere: in train stations, business offices, airports; English is the language of merchandise, and these days, merch is God. But back then, Latin was used for public announcements, while English remained the lingo of ragmen and roughnecks. And here was John, translating the Vulgate, the divine Latin of Saint Jerome, into British, the pidgin of lunkheads, not to mention refuting transubstantiation—what is he, crazy?—and sending his disciples, *the poor*, out to the sticks to spread his doctrine. He's been reading too much Augustine and Lactantius; his mind is gone. The Lollards propagated his ludicrous ideas about holy poverty, an egalitarian soup lapped up by the little bumpkins of Devon. On their dilapidated farms where their children were dropping like flies, it made sense to them, that direct relationship with God they were being told about, without the mediation of priests, or tithes, or the grand lifestyle of cardinals. This gospel poverty was their daily life!

"Leave everything and follow me," Christ is supposed to have said; the commandment is infinite, it demands a new humanity. Enigmatic and naked. It sweeps away the grandeurs of the world. One kind of poverty destroys, another exalts. There is a great mystery in that: To love the poor means to love baneful poverty, to stop despising it. It means to love mankind. For man is poor. Irremediably. *We* are poverty, buffeted between desire and disgust. At that moment in history, when Wycliffe sets in motion what will become the Reformation, God and the people speak the same language.

Naturally, Rome condemned John Wycliffe, and despite his profound and sincere words, he finished his days alone. More than forty years after his death, condemned by the Council of Constance, his body was exhumed and his bones reduced to ashes. Their loathing died hard.

———

For his words moved the poor and stirred up a great disorder. One of Wycliffe's disciples was a peasant named John Ball. We don't know when he was born, or anything about his parents, or much of anything about him. His traces are lost in the tide of ordinary fates. Around 1370, he began roving the fields, along verdant valleys, between hills. He went from farm to farm, hamlet to hamlet; he preached against the rich and powerful, talked to vagabonds, ne'er-do-wells, beggars. He versified and sowed his illicit beliefs along the way: "If God would have had any bondmen from the beginning, he would have appointed who should be bond, and who free," he declared, crisscrossing the countryside. He wandered, and the hinges of old thinking burst off the doors; and heigh 'neath the garlands of holly, and ho in the morning dew, shadow absorbed by shadow, on a rostrum of dung. He preached to jacks-of-all-trades, to poor wetnurses, to urchins, trembling all the while. His speeches were stitched together from everyday proverbs, common morality. But John Ball knew that the equality of souls had always existed in

the leafy thickets; he could feel it guiding him,
making proclamations. They nicknamed him the
ardent prior of the pickets; he was frightening.

In 1380, Parliament passed a new poll tax,
and suddenly the peasants revolted. The uprising
began in Brentwood: roads were blocked, castles
burned. Then it spread to Kent, Norfolk, and
Sussex. And John Ball ranted, preached human
equality. The inns were full of pilgrims and crack-
pots. In Colchester, among the bundles of wool
and strings of onions, people were talking; in East
Anglia, they were talking; everywhere, the poll tax
was questioned and hierarchies challenged. Noble-
men fled. Soldiers deserted. The village streets
were littered with wreckage, overturned carts,
sacks of earth. The powers that be were alarmed.
The Duke of Lancaster issued his orders: John
Ball must be placed under arrest. In May, they
managed to lay hands on the ardent prior and
imprison him in Maidstone.

It was then that another man awoke. Not very
far away in Kent, an ex-soldier who had served
in France went back to being a peasant. One

morning, the tax collector came for the tax. Wat
Tyler was out, having gone to the forest to chop
wood. His daughter answered the door, and the
man came into their home. He demanded their
contribution, but the girl couldn't pay him as they
had barely enough to live on. The tax collector
tore off her dress, threw her onto the straw mat,
and took his payment. She was fifteen. She was
pretty. She was virtue itself. But no one made a
virtue of poverty or of its children. Her lips turned
blue; she was cold. She staggered down the little
path bordered by blackberry bushes. Her father
saw her from a distance. Huge masses of clouds
skimmed the treetops. The deer's hide quivered.
Wat Tyler carried his daughter back home, hold-
ing her in his arms like a corpse. He entrusted
her to neighbors and ran off, ran across the hill,
hoping to catch up with the tax collector's car-
riage by cutting through the woods. He reached
the highway and crouched low, out of breath. He
wondered if the man had already passed by, but
moments later came the pounding of hooves. He
heard the plaintive call of the lark and felt himself

shed a cold tear. The horseman appeared. Wat Tyler burst onto the road, raised his arm, and struck. His mallet split the man's skull. The rider fell, the horse whinnied and swerved. Another blow, to the back, in the arid light of day, fractured his shoulder. All that remained of him was a lump of dead flesh.

Then the peasants of Kent rose up. Wat Tyler took the lead and the band headed toward Maidstone. There, what happened is not certain. The story goes that upon the insurgents' arrival, the Archbishop of Canterbury freed John Ball to pacify the crowd. But once freed, John Ball led his partisans to the archbishop's palace, which they sacked. Then they went to Lambeth. On the way, they took the archbishop captive, then proceeded to attack the Tower of London. Rain drenched their faces. The peasants marched in no particular order, and they were many, more than a hundred thousand. They came from everywhere, the impoverished masses banded together. A dog ran off under the sun, a woman went mad and started kissing everyone, a brute killed his master, holy water burned a child's face. In London, there was panic. The king didn't know what to do. Burghers and nobles wandered like shadows through the corridors. Whispers, cries. The paupers knocked down prison doors as they went, freed the captives, and men emerged from dungeons, eyes squeezed shut, unable to see. Old men and wraiths. They embraced them, gave them food and drink. They died. At least that's how the fable goes.

Furious, the peasants yanked judges from their beds, dragged them into the public square, and cut off their heads. The weather was lovely. A throng had gathered, panting and sweaty; never had anyone seen so many people. The Thames was shining, the water sparkling, screams filled the city and passed through the walls. Gulls flew overhead, but no one heard them. And Wat Tyler sent men to talk to the crowd and forbid looting under pain of death; he organized bivouacs. By day's end, a delegation was in place; the insurgents demanded to speak to the king. To the king? At that moment, he still seemed to be above any equality, a great amorphous countenance, the supreme authority. They appealed to him. He was the last guarantor of justice on earth, or so they believed. Wasn't it parliament that had voted for that diabolical poll tax? The king didn't want it, he would listen to the people, he would come to meet them on the shores of truth. But the king didn't come. And so the insurgents went deeper into London, fraternized with the population, harangued in the public squares, ran through the streets. Now they were demanding the abolition of serfdom. Might as well call for the downfall of society.

Nights abounded in celebration, alcohol, and music; the past seemed to melt away, and authority to crumble. They attacked the Savoy Palace, the most prestigious house in England, home of the Duke of Lancaster, the king's uncle, whom they accused of supporting the tax. The duke eluded the mob, but the palace was burned. Furnishings and tapestries were torn down and thrown into the Thames in a state of jubilation. Everything was reduced to ash. The king was fourteen years old; he took refuge in the Tower of London. They didn't know what to do.

From that point on, everything happened quickly. On June 13, the king tried to flee. He crossed the Thames in a boat, but in Greenwich the masses prevented him from landing. The next day he rode off on horseback, but they caught him at Mile End. There, he finally negotiated, granting them everything: freedom for the serfs, abolition of the tax, general amnesty for the rebels. But it was no longer enough. The rebels stormed the Tower of London. The Archbishop of Canterbury tried to escape. They immediately dragged him to the hill north of the tower and beheaded him. The houses bordering the square were silent; the windows were open, but no one made a sound. What had been immutable was now broken. Robert de Hales, the lord treasurer, was beheaded in turn, along with other high-placed personages. Each head was displayed on London Bridge, above the southern gatehouse, impaled on a pike.

The king resumes negotiations with Tyler, in Smithfield, where he repeats his promises. The rebels aren't buying it. They doubt the monarch's sincerity. Hasn't he tried twice to escape? But the king assures them that all their demands will be met. He is wearing a small blue cap, a gold tunic, and sporting handsome, flowing locks. The king is little more than a child. Wat Tyler hesitates. His comrades want guarantees. The barons flanking the king are hostile, the atmosphere is tense, the horses skittish. Suddenly, some troublemakers insult Tyler and try to knock him down. His horse swerves, a soldier pulls a dagger, and all hell breaks loose. A man is wounded, his leg spurts blood. Horses turn about, foaming, people jostle one another. Rocks fly. Faces are bathed in sunlight. A cloud passes. And suddenly William Walworth, the lord mayor, jabs his sword and injures Wat Tyler. Tyler's chest is soaked in red, a terrible red. His eyes roll back; time creeps forward in its tortoise shell. He falls from his horse, breaks his hip, his armor clanks. Everything explodes in a great commotion, shouts, bodies trampled, a horseman falls, then another. Then a rider comes up to Tyler, who is prostrate on the ground; they look at each other—all the kings of the earth whisper their simian breath into the rider's ear; eternity tries to close the locks, but the gate is open—and the rider finishes him off. Wat Tyler lies on the ground, disemboweled. Then everything speeds up even more. The king pushes the rebels back and speaks out: He embraces their cause and assures them of his support. They have nothing to fear—he swears it!—but they must disperse immediately. Fear and disorder do the rest. This huge crowd, come to London to fight, is suddenly overcome by a great, overpowering sadness. They no longer know who to listen to, and they disband. They head away from London in small groups, dreading the worst, dubious of the king's promises, not knowing what to do next.

One of the king's captains, Robert Knolles, is lying in wait outside the city. With his men, he swoops down on the rebels and slaughters them. And the reprisals are only beginning. The king himself leaves for Kent at the head of his regiment. Armed bands crisscross the countryside, tracking the now-dispersed insurgents, hunting them down like animals; many thousands of peasants are executed on the spot. The king revokes all his concessions. The repression is cold, intractable, and lasts nearly two months. John Ball is finally arrested and immediately hanged and quartered. There is no more talk of repealing the poll tax, and serfdom will not be abolished for another two hundred years.

And yet, it began anew. John Ball and Wat Tyler were reincarnated in Jack Cade. In 1450, he issued a manifesto, "The Complaint of the Poor Commons of Kent," and was given the nickname John Amend-all. That July, at the head of a band of five thousand men, peasants, artisans, decommissioned soldiers, and shopkeepers, Jack Cade took the Tower of London. They beheaded the Lord High Treasurer, they beheaded the former sheriff of Kent and several other individuals. The revolutionaries again entered London, and this time they pillaged the city. One evening, Jack Cade took shelter in a garden, a shadow came forward, a knife flashed in the dark, and the rebel was but a corpse. But it wasn't over yet. It started right up again in Sussex. John and William Merfold called for the murder of nobles and priests. That autumn, their men gathered, armed with bludgeons. At Robertsbridge, they prevented the clergy from collecting dues; in Eastbourne, they rebelled against inflated land rents. They challenged the social order. By dint of raids, militias, and hangings, their rebellion was put down.

IN BOHEMIA

And this wasn't the end of the story. It's never the end. The heart resumed beating in Bohemia; just after Wycliffe's was stilled in England, a certain Jan Hus took up his mantle and translated his *Trialogus* into Czech. And then he too began agitating. He preached in Bethlehem Chapel in Prague in favor of church reform. And off it went again: The pope issued a few more bulls that floated off toward Bohemia but snagged one by one on the little spires of Prague.

And now the pope called for a crusade against the king of Naples, and here was Jan Hus getting up on the pulpit of Bethlehem Chapel and preaching disobedience. He preached that one should love and pray even for the enemies of Christ, and thundered that true repentance could not be gained from buying indulgences, or from violent crusades, or from princely power. It was done. Again the words had been spoken: *not from money, or power, or princes.* Those same small words might change form and tone, but never their target. Each time they come back into the world, their struggle is always against money, influence, and power. Little by little, those words would become ours. They would take a long, long time to make their way to us. We still hear them, faintly, in Jan Hus's sermons, but perhaps they'd never been heard very clearly.

Then came the riots. The people rose up. Prague was in flames. The rioters were hunted down. Students burned the papal bulls, so they chopped up the students with axes. And then it all turned even uglier.

A general council was convened. At the time, three popes were laying claim to Peter's throne: the pope of Rome, the pope of Pisa, and the pope of Avignon. Gregory XII, John XXIII, and Benedict XIII. That's a lot of names and numbers to keep straight; it was complicated. And in the midst of this imbroglio, they fretted over Hus's body. The leading canonists knocked themselves out over it: Is Hus a heretic? Let's have a look at his liver, his gallbladder, his foreskin.

Yes, he is. No doubt about it. He said the host does not become flesh. Without further ado, they summoned him to Constance; then they threw him in jail, tried him, and burned him alive. He was coifed with a cardboard miter and bound to a stake. And Jan Hus burned, he burned like wood, like straw. He burned like the heart.

It was therefore in Bohemia, in the Bohemia of Jan Hus—nearly a century afterward, but the memory of it was still vivid and ideas make their way—that Thomas Müntzer the recalcitrant arrived. For twenty-five years, the rebellious population had stood against the allied European armies; for twenty-five years they had been Hussites, Taborites, fanatics of every stripe. Eighteen thousand men had died at the Battle of Lipany. For twenty-five years, they had relegated purgatory, revoked mortal sins, renounced the monarchy for the reign of God only. They had even demanded the end of the state and the redistribution of wealth. That's where things stood.

And Thomas Müntzer, as soon as he arrived, drafted his *Prague Manifesto*. He wrote it in German and had it translated into Czech. Müntzer rejected the debates among learned theologians; esotericism made him sick. He appealed to public opinion. It's one aspect of his greatness. The most profound theses demand to be known by everyone.

He expresses himself impulsively, in no particular order, following the burning thread of his desire. For Thomas Müntzer has one desire, and

the desire that makes you a cardinal is not the
same desire that makes you Thomas Müntzer.
Something terrible inhabits him, agitates him. He
is enraged. He wants the rulers' skins, he wants to
sweep away the church, he wants to gut all those
bastards. But maybe he doesn't know this yet,
and for the moment he is choking it down. He
wants to put an end to all that pomp and miserable circumstance. Vice and wealth devastate him;
their conjunction devastates him. He wants to
inspire fear. The difference between Müntzer and
Hus is that Müntzer is thirsty, hungry and thirsty,
terribly hungry and thirsty, and nothing can sate
him, nothing can slake his thirst. He'll devour old
bones, branches, stones, mud, milk, blood, fire.
Everything.

THE WHOLE WORLD

several months later, Thomas Müntzer left
Prague, and for a year and a half he led
an errant life. We have several letters from
that period, one to Philipp Melanchthon,
another to Martin Luther. The latter went unanswered. In it, Müntzer wrote with vigor, invoked
the living Word, a word that came not from books
but from the heart. God speaks, He addresses us
through the foliage and silhouettes of dreams.
But Müntzer's vehemence frightened off other

theologians. Carlstadt objected that it was very difficult to know God's will, that His Kingdom was not of this world, and kept his distance. By 1522, our little preacher was on his own. It was then that he settled in Allstedt, where he wrote his *Protestation*. In aggressive prose, he stated that the crucial experience of humanity was suffering. It alone permitted one to receive the word of God. It was the sickle that cleared out the soul, sliced through the weeds; and he called out to a bitter Christ. "Jezebel is not yet completely devoured by the dogs, she lives still, aye." That's what he wrote. The bitter Christ is his most abject image, and the most moving.

And then he sets his sights on reason. Enough with Erasmus! Enough with Seneca! You first have to be killed in order to be reborn. Müntzer goes overboard, he exults. For him, the spirit is the Cross. Life is the Cross. Truth is the Cross. Behind the rites, he wants to rediscover authentic suffering, primary clarity. For the soul is Christ. Yes, the little soul must, like Christopher Colum-bus, roam the world in search of God; it must scratch its knees on brambles, have its cheeks whipped by branches, its lungs flayed by the cold wind. He wants to purge himself of every sham, Thomas Müntzer. He wants to feel his little soul clean and tidy after all that soiling and suffering; to feel his body emerging into broad daylight.

He doesn't give a tinker's damn about ritual. Baptism, whether for adults or infants, he couldn't care less. The only baptism is spiritual. It is one's little soul that gets sprinkled with water, that stands on the ark in the flood, that slips out of Gomorrah at nightfall.

And Müntzer goes all out in his *Protestation*. He addresses Jews, heathens, Turks! He wants to convince them, convert them. He goes head-to-head with Islam, Judaism, heathenism. He writes for the whole world.

THE WORD

More than anything, Müntzer goes after Latin. He sets the simplicity of the common folk against Latin, and this simplicity is not vulgar, it can be converted. Mud is gold. And while Luther translates the Bible into German, Müntzer speaks to those who cannot read in their own language.

He goes further than Luther. In the church of Allstedt, God speaks German. The German Mass

ÉRIC VUILLARD

causes an uproar. People flock from miles around
Allstedt to hear the Word of God; crowds make
the long journey to hear a priest talk to them for
the first time in their language.

Immediately, enemies rear their heads. Count
Ernst von Mansfeld threatens to lock up any of
his subjects who go to Allstedt to hear Müntzer.
Because laborers, artisans, a whole population of
ignoramuses, and even some burghers are rushing
there. They want to hear the Word in German,
they want to know what someone has been telling
them all these years in that alien tongue; they're
sick of repeating *amen* and those incomprehensible
couplets. It is no insult to God to ask him politely
to speak our language.

Müntzer said Mass in German. And when
Count von Mansfeld forbade his subjects from
going to hear him, his tone changed, and another
Müntzer appeared: furious, wrathful, as they say
in bibles. He ratcheted up his rhetoric, and if we
don't carefully measure his next step, we won't understand a thing about fanaticism, we will only be
horrified. But if we properly gauge that step and

the reasons for it; if we fully appreciate how such an injunction can inflame the temper of a proud man, that is, a man who deems himself the equal of all others, then we can begin to understand something about this harder line, the pulsating folly that grips Müntzer's heart and causes him to sign his letter to the count *Destroyer of the faithless*.

THE SERMON TO
THE PRINCES

Yes, a furious, wrathful Müntzer ratchets things up. He writes to Prince Friedrich III, Elector of Saxony, the count's overlord; but no more dulcet tones, no more bowing and scraping. After invoking princes whose righteous actions are the only ones to fear, Müntzer raises his voice, now raises it more than one notch, raises it by once again climbing up his father's gibbet, where the rope is tied to the beam, to the very apex of misfortune and injustice, and from there, after inviting *His Highness* to condemn the path by which princes terrify the people rather than earn their love, he evokes the sword, threatening: "Princes should not terrify the pious. But if that does happen, then the sword will be taken away from them and given to the wrathful."

There it is: for perhaps the first time, it is heard. *The sword will be taken away from them and given to the wrathful.* How good that sounds, and how much good it does!

Not long afterward, he was summoned before Electoral Duke Johann, the crown prince, the bailiff, the burgomaster, and the council, so that they might gain a clearer idea of the doctrine of such a man. But instead of the expected self-justification, Müntzer began by commenting on a dream, and not just any dream, but Nebuchadnezzar's, in which Daniel announced to the king the end of his realm. The golden head falls. The feet of clay are crushed. All the kingdoms that follow Babylon will be destroyed, except for one. That one is indestructible, for it is the Kingdom of God.

The princes don't really care to hear about the destruction of kingdoms. The idea unsettles them. Nebuchadnezzar's dream is a prophecy of doom.

And Müntzer was not satisfied with a well-mannered exegesis; he raised the temperature still higher. He cited Matthew and John: "Every tree that does not bring forth good fruit should be uprooted and cast into the fire." He cited Luke: "Bring hither mine enemies, and slay them before me." He cited the Psalms: "The Lord will smash down the old pots of clay with his rod of iron." How violent he had suddenly become, how his gorge rose! And into that terrible diatribe he slipped a few jocular insults, with frightening seriousness. But more than anything, in lieu of God's good flocks that have been talked about since time immemorial—the good, silent flocks, pitiful and acquiescent, who are given their spray of holy

water—Müntzer introduced another populace,
more invasive and tumultuous, a real populace,
the poor laity and the peasants. This was a far cry
from the catechistic generality of kindly Christian
folk; now it was about ordinary people.

And those ordinary people stink, and grunt,
but they also think. So imagine, amid words
like *scoundrels, sword, ruins, slay them*, what a
dreadful impression the phrase *the poor laity and
the peasants* must have made. The princes were
not pleased. Then Müntzer comes to the end of
his sermon, where the expressions *wrath of God,
wrath of Christ, wrath of divine wisdom* appear
over and over. Facing this audience of grandees,
he evokes Absalom lost, pierced by javelins. The
nobles pull a face, but it gets worse: He denies
that anything can be changed *amicably*. No
doubt at that moment his mouth is twisted in a
grimace—*amicably*, no, that won't do, one needs
a trial by fire, he tells them, against those who are
offended by the slightest word of the Gospel. For
the powerful never give up anything, not bread
and not freedom. And at that moment, he speaks

before them his most terrible words. Before Duke Johann, the crown prince, the bailiff Zeiss, the burgomaster, and the Council of Allstedt; after the sword, the poor, Nebuchadnezzar, and the wrath of God, now Müntzer says: *Godless rulers should be killed.*

THE SUMMER IS
KNOCKING AT
OUR DOORS

und means mouth and *Zerstörung*, destruction. As such, we are free to hear, in Thomas Müntzer, a prodigious affinity between word and negation. Of course, we could see Müntzer as one of those passionate idealists whom the medical profession habitually ridicules. We could shove Rousseau, Tolstoy, and Lenin onto the couch and squeeze information out of them. We could see in any revolt and in any ardor a personal pain transfigured; what of it?

Suddenly, heads turn and bodies have the weightlessness of light. And then, anything can be said! Thoughts streak, draw together; those that leave no verbal trace fall away forever. They fall into the pit. We no longer hear them, no longer see them. We love them with remorse, and remorse is good for you. The great equality of the void.

Yes, Müntzer is violent; yes, Müntzer is a raving loon. He calls for the Kingdom of God here and now—there's impatience for you! The inflamed are like that: They spring forth one fine day from the head of the populace the way ghosts seep from walls.

But by what treasure of distance and delegation, by what twists and turns of the soul are the great sophisms of power maintained? One could write a history—nuanced, subtle, wildly improbable; but also shameful, with a thousand doses of poison, of lies proffered, fabricated, admitted, believed, repeated; of sincere prejudices, secret, half-avowed guilty consciences, and all the contortions of which the soul is capable.

Still, between two long periods of struggle, voices arise. The more regular the pain, the more staccato the voices. The more unanimous the authority, the more singular the voices. Müntzer is a voice. He cries out that, princes or servants, rich or poor, God molded us from the same gutter mud, whittled us from the same sandalwood.

Müntzer is a crackpot, fair enough. Sectarian. Yes. Messianic. Yes. Intolerant. Yes. Bitter. Perhaps. Alone. Sort of. Here's what he said: "Behold, I have put my words in your mouth; I have this day set you over the nations and over the kingdoms, to root out, and to pull down, and to destroy, and to throw down, to build, and to plant." And something else: "Try as they may to fight against you, a wonderful victory is prepared for the downfall of the strong and godless tyrants." And still more: "Dear brethren, stop your delaying and hesitating! The time has come, the summer is knocking at our doors. Do not keep friendship with the ungodly who prevent the Word from exercising its full force. Do not flatter your princes in order that you may not perish with them. Ye tender, bookish scholars, do not be wroth, for it is impossible for me to speak otherwise." As for us, what will be impossible?

THE INSURGENCY OF
ORDINARY MEN

The Peasants' War began in Swabia, near Lake Constance. Then it spread toward the Tyrol and the north. It was a succession of revolts, not only among peasants but also in the city, among workers. Müntzer had spoken to the poor, and for a while he tried to unite the discontented masses. He ordered Count von Mansfeld to "humble himself before the lowly." The count had never heard such a thing! Müntzer declared that all the birds of the sky shall devour the flesh of the princes. It's a quote from the Bible.

He signed his letters *Thomas Müntzer with the Sword of Gideon.* He went off the deep end. He believed himself inspired. He was. He was inspired by green leaves, dung, smallpox, clouds, by the great hive of cities, by his ideas of liberation, by the trampled fields, by smallholdings and estates, by uprooted vines, by tariffs, by charges, by insulting nicknames, by scythes, palings, spears; yes, he was inspired by the great rictus of the ailing beast, by the torn curtain, by salvos, workshops, routine labor, and heaps of facts; yes, he was inspired by God, but God is the real scar, the commerce of waves, "a blackened bundle of frustration and torpor."

It was while trying to organize a revolt in Thuringia, in Allstedt, that Müntzer broke away from the other preachers. Things acquired an undercurrent of societal rage. The well-to-do fringe of his sympathizers started to fret. He spoke of a world without privilege, property, or government.

He forcefully incited against oppression. He called Luther "the easy-living flesh of Wittenberg." He said, "All the world must suffer a big jolt." He said, "The lords themselves make the poor man their enemy. They cannot remove the cause of rebellion, so how can it turn out well in the long run? Oh, sires! How beautiful it will be to see the Lord smash down the old pots of clay with a rod of iron! That is what I say—and if that makes me a rebel, then so be it." And so it was.

On March 17, 1525, Mühlhausen rose up, mere days after Müntzer's arrival. He had not wanted this rebellion, which came too soon. But that's how facts are, they happen when they happen. Müntzer resigned himself. Since the revolt had started, he proclaimed, "Stir it up in the villages and especially amongst the miners and other good fellows who will be useful. We must sleep no longer." He encouraged Balthasar, Barthel Krump, Valentin, and Bischof to lead the way. The heart must become larger than all the castles, more solid than all the armor. Time to strike, while the iron is hot. "On, on, onwards!" he cried. "As long as they live, it is not possible to be emptied of the fear of man. You can be told nothing about God as long as they rule over you. On, onwards, while you have daylight. God marches before you, so follow, follow!"

At that point, Kurt von Tütcheroda joins him, Heinrich Hack joins him, Christoph von Altendorf joins him. And he writes letter upon letter; his is initially a war of words. Thomas Müntzer knows how to put pen to paper. There's something lively and fateful about him, an aroused hatred, a wicked turn of mind, but also gentleness. Nietzsche secretly took inspiration from him, from the Müntzeresque gush and extravagance. But Müntzer is a man of action; he gets carried along by his own prose. He does not despise the commoner, the ordinary man. Müntzer is daffodil and thistle, nettle and sap. He quotes Daniel: "Power will be given to the people." We're a long way from Nietzsche.

The revolt grinds on. In Hesse, in Upper Franconia, in Thuringia, in the Harz Mountains, in Saxony, from all corners, people are jostling, pushing, and shoving one another. Mühlhausen and Erfurt are at the heart of this popular uprising. Castles are razed, ramparts smashed; everywhere people are saying that the peasants are revolting, that they're going all the way to Rome. They say that people are rising up even on the outer fringes of Christendom, even among the Turks!

At first, the princes don't know what to do; the world seems to breathe faster, it is perpetual daylight, birds eat dirt, beasts sleep on the hoof. The Landgrave of Hesse, Philipp I the Magnanimous, is twenty years old; he is a clever lad, but self-centered and untutored. A nasty mug has young Philipp, and the very fine portrait of him from about ten years later—a painting that is now in a corner of the Wartburg Museum, beneath an overly bright window—shows a bulging forehead, protruding eyes, a pained scowl, and greasy skin.

Around 1504, just as Philipp was coming into the world, but very far away from there, in Cathay, the good Shen Zhou was painting oranges and chrysanthemums. He had first painted them in his mind, petal by petal, peel by peel, quarter by quarter, pit by pit. And that day, as he was painting them on a long textile scroll, there was a light, chill wind. On November 13, 1504, his scroll of ink and pale colors folded in on itself. The birds flew off into the landscape, the solitary fisherman raised his head, the chestnuts fell into the water, the boat drifted a moment from shore. And in the tall grass sprouting among the rocks, between the dead branches, the little crab of time came to tickle the painter's fingers. Shen Zhou was old. Sitting by the river, he felt some of his sap and strength drain away from him; the disk of the moon sank into the pail. A few touches of gray and black were added, a leaf curled up. His training as a painter had been slow, and late in life his death would be gentle. He had painted

landscapes, flowers, animals, and he passed away
in a forest of saplings. At that moment, thousands of miles away, Philipp of Hesse, I mean the
five-year-old who would become the Landgrave of
Hesse, felt a strange shiver, like a surge of anteced-
ence. A branch scraped the wall, the night moved.
And even if you don't give a shit whether or not
the Chinese painter of rocks and birds had some
mysterious kinship of the soul with the Landgrave
of Hesse, fantasies are nonetheless one path to the
truth. History is Philomela, and they raped her,
or so they say, and cut out her tongue, and she
whistles at night from deep in the woods.

Faced with this upheaval, the Landgrave of
Hesse didn't know what to think. He was
young and impetuous. He paced round and
round Luther's room, where the great man had
lodged, and through the small window gazed at
the rooftops of Wartburg. The sun was out. The
countryside was all in green, and smoke no longer

poured from the chimneys. The town was big and pretty enough, but from above, like this, that day, it seemed to him that a kind of light fog was hovering over it, a halo; he couldn't say what it was.

Still, the prince had to decide, so as not to leave Müntzer time to organize; since the month of April, he'd had an army. He had ordered expeditions throughout his territory and quashed several rebellions. On May 3, he had beaten the peasants from Fulda. Still, he hesitated. Should he march on Mühlhausen? Should he defy Müntzer?

In Mühlhausen, Müntzer was occupied with reforms; but the revolt ended in a petty democracy of artisans. His companions from Allstedt joined him, and he immediately began preaching to the weavers of Mühlhausen, the miners of Mansfeld: "Anyone who has a desire to fight against the Turk does not have far to go: he is here on our doorsteps.... The princes' souls are in peril, for God wants them pulled out by the root!" But even that tone no longer sufficed; it didn't enflame enough people, didn't move fast enough. And so, when Müntzer learned that a crowd was rebelling in Frankenhausen, and that its numbers were swelling as the neighboring peasants poured in, he called upon the town of Sondershausen to rise up. "Attack the eagle's nest!"

The threat became clearer; the princes banded together. The Landgrave of Hesse cut off all connection between Frankenhausen and other groups of peasants in Franconia. On March 12, 1525, Müntzer took to the roads. He had with him three hundred men, no more, like Gideon. He believed he was reenacting the fable. He was going to war, as in the Bible, praying, exulting, calling for a miracle, in an atmosphere of Doomsday.

LAST LETTERS

After that, everything happened fast. Müntzer had no cavalry, no artillery. Just a few bombards. Opposite him: six princely columns, well organized, well trained, and well fed. New reinforcements of insurgents headed toward them, but the princes cut them off. It was then that Count Albrecht von Mansfeld initiated negotiations. It was important that these talks drag on, in order to demoralize the adversary and gain time. Negotiations are a means of combat.

Albrecht von Mansfeld bore the number 7, as the seventh Albrecht in his family. There had already been six Albrechts. I don't know anything about Albrechts 5 or 6, but Albrecht 4 was a good egg; he died at the age of forty, toothless and happy. As for Albrecht 3, not much to say: his existence is disputed; some claim that he was actually called Gerhard or Abdel, which is flatly impossible. And Albrecht 2? Or 1? Hard to tell—you can get lost in the houses of Ascania, Henneberg, and Mecklenburg. But as for Albrecht 7, he was a wily one, he knew how negotiations should stretch out over time, so that the masters could regroup their forces. And besides, waiting saps the morale of those who are not used to war, and inclines them toward compromise. Not to mention that, since the beginning of their existence, they have been trained to feel so much respect, so much fear, that they're still willing to take a prince at his word, at least for a while. We always want to believe what the father says. Our desire is attuned to his register.

Müntzer was suspicious of the negotiations, smelling a trap. To break the spell in which the princes were trying to enclose him, he sent a letter to Count von Manderscheid, one of Albrecht's advisers—a poison-pen letter: "Have you not been able to taste in your Martin's manure what Ezekiel said in the 39th chapter, that God would command all the birds of the air to feast on the flesh of the princes and commanded the unthinking beasts to lap up the blood of the big-wigs, as is described in the secret Revelations 18 and 19?" Later in the letter, he wrote, citing Daniel, that "God has given power to the common people"; and he signed it *Thomas Müntzer with the Sword of Gideon.* He laid it on thick. No doubt he was deliberately trying to offend the count, foil his strategy of attrition by goading him into a fight. That's what Kautsky claims. Bloch thinks so, too. Engels says nothing. And on that point, God has kept silent.

Nor did Müntzer forget Count Ernst, who had issued the injunction against Masses in German. In one of several letters to him, Müntzer wrote:

"Now tell us, you miserable, wretched sack of maggots"—that's how he began—"who made you into a prince over the people whom God redeemed with his own blood?" Things were off to a good start, since it's always beneficial to hear the truth. Later, he added: "If you will not humble yourself before those of low standing, know that we have been given immediate orders, I say this to you: The eternal living God has commanded that you be cast down from your throne by the power given to us; for you are of no use to Christianity, you are a pernicious scourge of the friends of God.... Your nest must be ripped apart and destroyed. We want to have your answer by this evening, or else we will not hesitate to carry out what God has commanded us. So do your best. I am coming for you."

The two letters were delivered. And left unanswered.

WORDS

Meanwhile, the men were getting restless, caught as they were between Müntzer's fiery rhetoric and the princes' cavalry. At the same time, other troops were heading for Frankenhausen; the situation grew more dire with each passing day.

It was then that Philipp of Hesse arrived with an army of eight hundred cavalrymen and three thousand foot soldiers. All at once there

were defections among Müntzer's forces, and
they reconsidered negotiating. They were afraid,
and rightly so. Intense diplomatic activity began,
a deft and odious process of smoking out. The
princes demanded that Müntzer and his closest
associates be handed over. At this point, the story
gets murky, and all we can find, reported in the
writings of the false Melanchthon, are the imbe-
cilic declarations of a pseudo-Müntzer. What did
he really say? What did they really do? We can
guess. Müntzer must have blazed white-hot during
those several days. He must have gone off like a
firecracker, bellowed his faith and brought to bear
misery, rage, despair, and hope. The speeches at-
tributed to the princes, for their part, are patently
fake. They say that the truth has several faces, one
of which is more horrible than lies, but is always
hidden. It's strange to think that those scribblers
in their red caps deliberately erased the memory
of the ones being persecuted, that they agreed to
write falsely.

Still, even a false word will convey a flash of
truth between the lines. "It is not the peasants

who arose against you masters, but God himself!"
Luther reportedly said at first, in an admiring but
horrified cry. But it wasn't God. It was indeed the
peasants rising up. Unless you want to define God
as hunger, disease, humiliation, rags. It wasn't
God rising up, it was taxes, tithes, land rights,
ground rents, tariffs, travel dues, hay harvests,
droit du seigneur, cutting of noses, gouging of eyes,
pinching with burning tongs, bodies broken on
the wheel. In reality, quarrels about the Beyond
have to do with the world here-below. That's all
the influence that those aggressive theologies still
exert over us. The only reason for understanding
their verbiage. Their impetuousness is a violent
expression of poverty. The plebeians rebel. Hay for
the peasants! Coal for the laborers! Dust for the
road workers! Coins for the beggars! And words
for us! Words, which are another convulsion of
things.

THE BATTLE OF
FRANKENHAUSEN

A nd so, from the four corners of the
empire surged the destitute hordes.
Müntzer called out, and the crowds
came. The Landgrave of Hesse
couldn't believe his eyes. Urban laborers came,
madmen came; the peasants rose up en masse.
There was great terror among the nobles and
burghers. Women abandoned hearth and home,
children marched across the fields in pursuit of
the Holy Spirit. Young women, vagabonds, the

wretched rabble, even beasts! The gentry saw all
kinds of people going by, in twos or threes or
else alone, having left without baggage, without
anything. No one knew what they were after.
The lords and their armed gangs didn't dare lift a
finger; horrified, they watched the throngs pass by.
A vague fear began to rise. What should they do
now? No one had ever seen such a sight. Everyone was vacating house or shack and joining the
wandering horde. And where were all those people
going? No one knew. They were too frightening
to even try to disperse. They slept in the woods, in
the hay, dreaming.

But once the first moment of stupor had passed,
the princes reacted; they ordered their forces to
regroup. Several thousand well-armed, battle-
hardened men. The others, the ragged masses, had
loosely gathered in a huge plain, and there they
stood, no one really knowing what was what.

First there was a shout. Several horsemen
broke through the ranks of the disordered mob,
then their horses halted between the two camps.
It rained lightly. People took shelter beneath tall

dead trees. The soldiers were sweating in their iron carapaces. From afar, they saw a few silhouettes moving among the peasants.

Suddenly, there was a rumble in the left wing— nothing much, mind you, but a tremor that spread from animal to animal, rider to rider, like a gentle breeze in straw. One horse must have jostled another and a few men now lay fallen on the ground. Count Albrecht made a sign for them to wait. The ranks slackened. You could hear the clank of weapons. Everyone was at the ready. In the distance, the band of vagabonds did not seem to be preparing for the attack; their disorder was such that they must have had neither plan nor leader. The peasants hesitated to surrender. Their artillerymen didn't even get around to loading their bombards. There was total confusion. Just then, a rainbow appeared. The great bald cliff shone iridescent. The sky turned deep blue. Müntzer saw in this the sign he'd been waiting for. He spoke. They listened. Like so many before him, he invoked a sign. He saw the mark of

God. It was the moment of truth: They were about to cross the Jordan.

Then they began to pray, but not on their knees—standing. It must have been odd, those thousands of men wearing rags and bearing weapons, eyeing the heavens. Then, while still awaiting the reply of a final legation, the princes' artillery opened fire.

The pandemonium defies description. Bodies were struck and fell. There were shouts, smoke, people running for their lives. The volleys began again. The peasants ran wildly, cut down by flying lead. In the princes' camp, the infantry had taken position behind the crossbows and awaited their orders. The cavalry waited, too. Müntzer exhorted his men, screamed his confidence in God, tried to grab them by the sleeve, I don't know what he did, probably he shed tears, he raged. Bodies moaned in the grass, crying out, begging for help. The tall trees raised their arms in impotence. The sky was now a vast, horrible blue. At that moment, they heard another shout, or rather a scream, a hue and cry. It was the infantry and cavalry charging. The peasants in the first ranks, who until then had held firm, were swept aside.

Opposite them, several horsemen fell, slashed at by scythes. They were set upon, bits of their armor torn away, then left to be trampled or crushed under the bellies of their mounts. But the bulk of the troops pierced the peasants' front lines. The peasants managed to resist in two or three places. They formed small, compact knots, harassing the horses, yanking at an armband, a greave, a whatever, pulling in all directions until the rider fell and they slaughtered him.

Still, the cavalry's armaments gave them such an advantage that before long all resistance caved. Later, Philipp of Hesse would write: "We pursued with our troops, killing those who were wounded. We stormed the city immediately and conquered it. All the men to be found were put to death; the city was plundered and *with God's help* we were granted victory this day, for which we rightly give thanks to the Almighty in the hope of having accomplished and performed a charitable deed." There were four thousand casualties.

MÜNTZER BEHEADED

We want stories; we say they illuminate; and the truer the story, the better we like it. But no one knows how to tell true stories. And yet we're made of stories, we've been captivated by them since childhood: "Listen! Read! Look!"—our truth be done, may it draw us near and send us far with pictures and words.

———

Concerning the end of Thomas Müntzer, there exists a legend of cowardice with many variants. Müntzer supposedly fled and hid and they found him and turned him over to Count von Mansfeld and he was imprisoned in a dungeon and tortured and supposedly he recanted and implored the princes for mercy and dictated a contrite letter to the inhabitants of Mühlhausen. I don't believe a word of it. These scurrilous legends come along to bow the heads of renegades only after they have been denied the right to speak. Their sole purpose is to make the tormenting voice sound within us, the voice of order, to which we are ultimately so attached that we surrender to its mysteries and hand it our lives.

Müntzer was married; about his wife, we know almost nothing. We know she had been a nun, then had embraced his cause, and that after the disaster, after the wooden horse and gouging of eyes, her life was spared. They say, too, that she was pregnant at the time and that she was beaten and molested. We know of only one letter from her, a plea: "I humbly implore Your Princely Grace to please consider my great misery and poverty. I've heard it said that Your Princely Grace thought it wise for me to return to the convent. This is the favor I implore." Ernst Bloch has written that this letter is riddled with inconsistencies. Personally, I find it heartrending.

They also say that Müntzer had children. To avoid persecution, they had to change their names and adopt the diminutive Münzel, which means "small change," "alms."

And now, here is Thomas Müntzer, in the same spot as his father. Surely it was terrible to find himself there at the end, chained, in the midst of a crowd. I don't know what he was thinking about. I reject doubt, treachery, renunciation. It hardly matters. Because he was so bad at hating, because he had sought the reasons for his existence so far from himself and transmuted his hatred into bitter faith, because he had so strongly felt the power of the = sign, and because one does not get bread or freedom except by grabbing it, he found himself there.

I won't delve any further into his thoughts; I leave them to him. Here he is before us, on the scaffold, a million miles from retentive pleasure. I see him. Thomas Müntzer! And he is no longer the little Thomas of before, he is no longer the street urchin of the Harz Mountains, the son of the dead man, no longer even an object of study; he is any man, any fleeting life.

He is going to die now. He is going to die. He is thirty-five. His anger brought him here. All the way here. They have mangled his body, his arms, his legs; he's bleeding. He is worn out.

Then the blade rises. Faces are there in the hundreds, all around. They watch, stunned, not sure they're seeing right. The beggars, the tanners, the reapers, the poor sods watch, they watch! And what do they see? They see a small man under a great burden. They see a man like them, his body shackled. How small a man is, how fragile and violent, inconstant and severe, energetic and full of anguish. A look. A face. Skin. Suddenly the

blade falls and slices his neck. Oh! How heavy
a head is, a good several pounds of bone and
jelly. And how the blood spurts! His head will
be impaled. His body will be dragged over the
scaffold and thrown to the dogs. Youth is endless,
the secret of our equality immortal, and solitude
wonderful. Martyrdom is a trap for the oppressed.
Only victory is desirable. I shall tell of it.

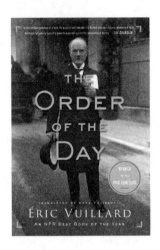

ISBN 978-1-63542-040-1

ENJOY THIS EXCERPT FROM

The

ORDER

of the

DAY

Éric Vuillard

Translated from the French by Mark Polizzotti

A SECRET MEETING

*T*he sun is a cold star. Its heart, spines of ice. Its light, unforgiving. In February, the trees are dead, the river petrified, as if the springs had stopped spewing water and the sea could swallow no more. Time stands still. In the morning, not a sound, not even birdsong. Then an automobile, and another, and suddenly footsteps, unseen silhouettes. The play is about to begin, but the curtain won't rise.

It's Monday. The city is just beginning to stir behind its scrim of fog. People go to work as on any other day; they board the bus or trolley, thread their way onto the upper deck, then daydream in the chill. And even though the twentieth of February 1933 was not just any other day, most people spent the morning grinding away, immersed in the great, decent fallacy of work, with its small gestures that enfold a silent, conventional truth and reduce the entire epic of our lives to a diligent pantomime. The day passed, quiet and normal. And while everyone shuttled between house and factory, market and courtyard where the laundry is hung out to dry, or in the evening between office and tavern, before finally heading home—far away, far from the decent labors, far from domestic life, on the banks of the Spree, some men got out of their cars in front of a palace. Through doors obsequiously held open, they stepped from their huge black sedans and paraded in single file, dwarfed by the heavy sandstone columns.

There were twenty-four of them, near the dead trees on the bank: twenty-four overcoats in black, brown, or amber; twenty-four pairs of wool-padded shoulders; twenty-four three-piece suits, and the same number of pleated trousers with wide cuffs. The shadows entered the large vestibule of the palace of the President of the Assembly—though before long, there would be no more assembly, no more president, and eventually no more parliament. Only a heap of smoking rubble.

For now, they doffed twenty-four felt hats and uncovered twenty-four bald pates or crowns of white hair. They shook hands solemnly before mounting the stage. The venerable patricians stood in the huge vestibule, exchanging casual, respectable banter, as if at the starchy opening of a garden party.

The twenty-four silhouettes conscientiously took a first stairway, then trudged up another flight, step after step, occasionally halting so as not to overtax their old hearts. They climbed, hands gripping the copper rail, eyes half-shut, without admiring the elegant banister or the vaulting, as if on a heap of invisible dead leaves. At the narrow entrance, they were ushered to the right; and there, after several paces over the checkered tiles, they scaled the thirty steps leading to the third floor. I don't know who was first in line, and ultimately it doesn't matter: all twenty-four had to do exactly the same thing, follow the same path, turn right around the stairwell, until finally, on their left, they entered the salon through the wide-open doors.

They say that literature gives you license. So I could, for instance, make them turn around the Penrose stairs in perpetuity, going neither up nor down, or both at the same time. And indeed, that's pretty much the sense we get from books. The time of words—compact or fluid, dense or impenetrable, stretched out, granular—halts movement and leaves us mesmerized. Our heroes are in the palace for all eternity, as if in an enchanted castle. They are thunderstruck from the outset, petrified, frozen. The doors are simultaneously open and shut, the fanlights worn, dangling, smashed, or repainted. The stairwell gleams, but it is empty; the chandelier sparkles, but it is dead. We are everywhere in time. And so, Albert Vögler climbed the steps to the first landing, and there he raised his hand to his detachable collar, sweating, dripping with perspiration, feeling slightly dizzy. Beneath the large gilded lantern that lit the flights of stairs, he straightened his vest, undid a button, loosened his collar. Perhaps Gustav Krupp paused on the landing as well, giving Albert a compassionate word, a small apothegm on old age—showed a little solidarity, in short. Then Gustav went on his way and Albert Vögler remained there a few moments longer, alone beneath the chandelier: a huge, gold-plated vegetable with an enormous ball of light in the center.

Finally, they entered the small salon. Wolf-Dietrich, private secretary to Carl von Siemens, dawdled for a moment near the French windows, letting his eyes linger on the thin coat of frost dusting the balcony. For a moment he escaped from the petty intrigues of this world, borne on cotton wool. And while the others chitchatted and puffed on their Montecristos, jabbering about the cream or taupe color of the wrappers and whether they liked their cigars smooth or spiced (though all of them were partial to fat ring gauges), absently squeezing the fine gold bands—while all of this was happening, Wolf-Dietrich stood daydreaming at the window, wavering with the bare branches and floating above the Spree.

A few steps away, admiring the delicate plaster figurines decorating the ceiling, Wilhelm von Opel raised and lowered his thick round glasses. His family was among those that had risen over the generations, going, through promotions and accumulations of estates and grandiose titles, from small landowners around the municipality of Braubach to magistrates, then burgomasters, until Adam Opel—issued from his mother's indecipherable entrails and schooled in the tricks of the locksmith's trade—designed a marvelous sewing machine that marked the true onset of their glory. In reality, Adam invented nothing. He got himself hired by a manufacturer, kept a low profile, then made a few improvements. He married Sophie Scheller, who brought with her a substantial dowry, and named his first sewing machine after her. At that point, production soared. It took only a few years for the sewing machine to realize its potential, enter the mainstream, become part of everyday life. Its true inventors had come along too early. Once the success of his sewing machines was a fait accompli, Adam Opel branched off into velocipedes. But one night, a strange voice slipped through the half-open door. His heart felt cold, so cold. It wasn't the sewing machine's actual inventors come to beg for royalties, or his workers demanding their share of the profits. It was God claiming his soul: he had to give it back.

But companies don't die like men. They are mystical bodies that never perish. The Opel brand continued selling bicycles, then automobiles. Already at its founder's death, the firm counted fifteen hundred employees, and it kept growing. A company is a person whose blood rushes to the head. We call these *legal entities*. Their lives last much longer than ours. And so, on this twentieth of February, as Wilhelm ruminated in the small salon of the palace of the President of the Reichstag, the Opel company was already an old lady. By now it was just an empire within another empire, bearing only a distant relation to Adam the patriarch's sewing machines. And though the Opel company was a very wealthy dowager, she was nonetheless so elderly that almost no one noticed her anymore; she had faded into the landscape. By now, the Opel company was older than many states, older than Lebanon, older than Germany itself, older than most African nations, older even than Bhutan, where the gods became lost in the clouds.

MASKS

One by one, then, we could approach all twenty-four of these gentlemen as they enter the palace, flit past their collar studs and the knots of their ties, lose ourselves an instant in the trim of their mustaches, zone out among the pinstripes of their jackets, plunge into their sad eyes. And there, deep inside that yellow, bristly arnica flower, we would always find the same little door; we would pull the bell cord and be transported back in time to witness the same string of underhanded maneuvers, marriages of convenience, double dealings—the tedious saga of their exploits.

By that February 20, Wilhelm *von* Opel, Adam's son, had brushed the motor grease from beneath his fingernails once and for all, put away his bike, left behind his sewing machine, and now sported a nobiliary particle that encapsulated his entire family history. From the height of his sixty-two years, he cleared his throat and glanced at his watch, then looked around him with pinched lips. Hjalmar Schacht had done his job well; he would soon be appointed Director of the Reichs-bank and Minister of the Economy. Around the table were Gustav Krupp, Albert Vögler, Günther Quandt, Friedrich Flick, Ernst Tengelmann, Fritz Springorum, August Rosterg, Ernst Brandi, Karl Büren, Günther Heubel, Georg von Schnitzler, Hugo Stinnes Jr., Eduard Schulte, Ludwig von Winterfeld, Wolf-Dietrich von Witzleben, Wolfgang Reuter, August Diehn, Erich Fickler, Hans von Loewenstein zu Loewenstein, Ludwig Grauert, Kurt Schmitt, August von Finck, and Dr. Stein. We're at the nirvana of industry and finance. There they sat, silent, well-mannered, and a little numb from having waited for almost twenty minutes. The smoke from their stogies made their eyes water.

As if in meditation, several shadows paused at a mirror and straightened their ties, making themselves at home in the small salon. Somewhere, in one of his four volumes on architecture, Palladio rather nebulously defines a salon as a living room, the stage on which we play out the vaudeville of our existence. And in the celebrated Villa Godi Malinverni, starting from the Olympus Room, where nude gods cavort among the trompe l'oeil ruins, through the Room of Venus, where a child and a page escape through a painted false door, you arrive at the Main Hall, where you find, on an architrave above the entrance, the end of a prayer: "And deliver us from evil." But in the palace of the President of the Assembly, where our little gathering was being held, you would have searched in vain for such an inscription: it was not on the program. Not the order of the day.

A few more minutes dragged by beneath the tall ceiling. They exchanged smiles. They opened leather briefcases. Now and again, Schacht raised his gold-rimmed spectacles and rubbed his nose, tongue at the edge of his lips. The guests remained quietly seated, training their crab-like eyes on the door. Whispers between two sneezes. A handkerchief was unfolded, nostrils honked in the silence; then they shifted in their seats, waiting patiently for the meeting to begin. They were old hands at meetings. All of them sat on various boards of directors or of trustees; all were members of some employers' association or other. Not to mention the sinister family reunions of this austere and stultifying patriarchy.

In the front row, Gustav Krupp fanned his rubicund face with his glove, hawked conscientiously into his hanky: he had a cold. With age, his thin lips were beginning to form a nasty inverse crescent. He looked sad and worried. Mechanically he twisted a beautiful gold ring, through the fog of his hopes and calculations—and it's possible that, for him, those two words had but a single meaning, as if they'd been magnetically drawn together.

*S*uddenly, the doors creaked, the floorboards groaned; sounds of talking in the anteroom. The twenty-four lizards rose to their hind legs and stood stiffly. Hjalmar Schacht swallowed his saliva; Gustav adjusted his monocle. Behind the door panels, they heard muffled voices, then a whistle blast. And finally, the President of the Reichstag, Hermann Goering himself, strode smiling into the room. This was no surprise, really, just an everyday occurrence. In the grand scheme of business, partisan struggles didn't amount to much. Politicians and industrialists routinely dealt with each other.

Goering went around the table with a word for everyone present, seizing each hand in a debonair grip. But the President of the Reichstag had not come merely to welcome them. He mumbled a few words of greeting, then immediately launched into the upcoming elections, on March 5. The twenty-four sphinxes listened closely. The electoral campaign would be crucial, the President of the Reichstag announced. It was time to get rid of that wishy-washy regime once and for all. Economic activity demanded calm and stability. The twenty-four gentlemen nodded solemnly. The electric candles of the chandelier blinked; the great sun painted on the ceiling shone brighter than before. And if the Nazi Party won the majority, added Goering, these would be the last elections for ten years—even, he added with a laugh, for a hundred years.

A wave of approbation swept over the seats. At that moment, there was a sound of doors, and the new chancellor finally entered the room. Those who had never met him were curious to see him in person. Hitler was smiling, relaxed, not at all as they had imagined: affable, yes, even friendly, much friendlier than they would have thought. For everyone present, he had a word of thanks, a dynamic handshake. Once the introductions had been made, everyone again took their comfortable chairs. Krupp was in the first row, picking at his tiny mustache with a nervous finger. Right behind him, two directors of IG Farben, along with von Finck, Quandt, and some others, sagely crossed their legs. There was a cavernous cough. The cap of a pen produced a minuscule clink. Silence.

They listened. The basic idea was this: they had to put an end to a weak regime, ward off the Communist menace, eliminate trade unions, and allow every entrepreneur to be the führer of his own shop. The speech lasted half an hour. When Hitler had finished, Gustav stood up, took a step forward, and, on behalf of all those present, thanked him for having finally clarified the political situation. The chancellor made a quick lap around the table on his way out. They

congratulated him courteously. The old industrialists
seemed relieved. Once he had departed, Goering took
the floor, energetically reformulating several ideas,
then returned to the March 5 elections. This was a
unique opportunity to break out of the impasse they
were in. But to mount a successful campaign, they
needed money; the Nazi Party didn't have a blessed
cent and Election Day was fast approaching. At that
moment, Hjalmar Schacht rose to his feet, smiled at
the assembly, and called out, "And now, gentlemen,
time to pony up!"

Cavalier though it was, the invitation was hardly
novel to these men, who were used to kickbacks and
backhanders. Corruption is an irreducible line item in
the budget of large companies, and it goes by several
names: lobbying fees, gifts, political contributions.
Most of the guests immediately handed over hundreds
of thousands of marks. Gustav Krupp gave a million,
Georg von Schnitzler four hundred thousand, and so
they raked in a hefty sum. That meeting of February
20, which might seem to us a unique moment in cor-
porate history, an unprecedented compromise with

the Nazis, was in fact nothing more for the Krupps, Opels, and Siemenses than a perfectly ordinary business transaction, your basic fund-raising. All would survive the regime and go on to finance many other parties, commensurate with their level of performance.

But to truly understand the meeting of February 20, 1933, to grasp its everlasting import, we must now call these men by their real names. It was not Günther Quandt, Wilhelm von Opel, Gustav Krupp, and August von Finck who were present that late afternoon, in the palace of the President of the Reichstag. We must use other designations. For "Günther Quandt" is a cryptonym; it masks something very different from the corpulent gentleman slicking down his mustache and sitting quietly in his seat around the table of honor. Close behind him is a rather more imposing silhouette, a tutelary shadow, as cold and impervious as a stone statue. Yes, hovering in all its fierce, anonymous power above Quandt and making him look stiff as a mask (but a mask that fits his face more closely than his own skin), we can see Accumulatoren-Fabrik AG, later called Varta—for as we know, legal entities have their avatars, just as ancient divinities took various forms and occasionally absorbed other divinities.

This, then, is the Quandts' real name, their demigod identity; whereas he, Günther, is but a tiny little mound of skin and bone like you and me. When he's gone, his sons will sit on the throne, then the sons of his sons. But the throne itself remains, even after the little mound of skin and bone has curdled in the earth. As such, these twenty-four men are not called Schnitzler, or Witzleben, or Schmitt, or Finck, or Rosterg, or Heubel, as their identity papers would have us believe. They are called BASF, Bayer, Agfa, Opel, IG Farben, Siemens, Allianz, Telefunken. By these names we shall know them. In fact, we know them very well. They are here beside us, among us. They are our cars, our washing machines, our household appliances, our clock radios, our homeowner's insurance, our watch batteries. They are here, there, and everywhere, in all sorts of guises. Our daily life is theirs. They care for us, clothe us, light our way, carry us over the world's highways, rock us to sleep.